Bullies
and Gangs

© Aladdin Books Ltd 2007

Designed and produced by
Aladdin Books Ltd
2/3 Fitzroy Mews
London W1T 6DF

First published in 2007
by Franklin Watts
338 Euston Road
London NW1 3BH

Franklin Watts Australia
Level 17/207 Kent Street
Sydney NSW 2000

Franklin Watts is a division of Hachette Children's Books.

ISBN 978 0 7496 7494 6

A catalogue record for
this book is available
from the British Library.

Illustrator: Christopher O'Neill

The author, Julie Johnson, is a health education consultant and trainer,
working with parents, teachers, carers and organisations such as Kidscape.

Dewey Classification:
362.7

Printed in China
All rights reserved

THOUGHTS AND FEELINGS

Bullies and Gangs

Julie Johnson

Aladdin / Watts
London • Sydney

Contents

Introduction

Have you ever been bullied? Would you know what to do if you saw someone being bullied? The children in this book know what it is like to be bullied and have some good tips on how to deal with bullying.

What Is Bullying?

Connie and Gary are talking about different kinds of bullying. Connie knows bullying can be about physically hurting someone. Gary says it can also be calling someone rude names or saying horrible things about them. Taking or hurting someone's property can also be bullying. Have any of these things ever happened to you?

Stealing can be bullying.

Bullying isn't just hitting someone.

Calling people names is bullying, too.

Why do they always pick on me?

▶ Just A Game

It is good to be part of a group having fun, as long as everyone is enjoying what is going on. But it's not fun if you get hurt, or aren't enjoying the game. It's not fun if one person is being picked on to give everyone else a good time.

Give me the money, or there'll be trouble.

◀ Money Or Else...

Bullying is something that happens in every school. Some bullies pick on people who are smaller than they are. They may demand your money or belongings, and threaten to hit you if you don't give them what they want. This is wrong, it is stealing.

▶ Scared To Tell

Some bullies work in gangs. They may make fun of how you look or the clothes you wear.

They may threaten to hurt you if you tell anyone. Bullies rely on people being too scared to say what is going on.

Story: Scott Pretends

1 Scott picked on Ben in the playground at lunchtime.

2 Ben was too frightened to tell anyone that he was being bullied.

3 Mrs Thomas saw the boys and came over to see what was happening.

Do you think Scott was just playing?

No. It's not playing if someone scares you, or makes you do anything you don't want to do. Mrs Thomas noticed Scott threatening Ben. Bullies pick a place where they think they won't get caught. Bullying can happen in the playground, the school corridors or toilets, or outside the school. Bullying can happen at home. Wherever it happens, it is wrong.

> They never let me join in.

▶ Is Bullying Easy To Spot?

It is easy to spot that bullying is going on if someone is being hit or pushed around. But some kinds of bullying are less obvious. Deliberately leaving someone out of a game and never letting them join in is bullying, too.

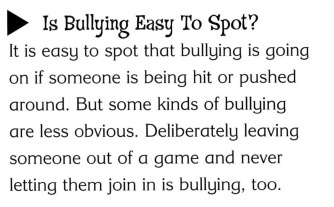

▶ Taking Your Friends Away...

Some bullies may even try to take your friends away, so that it is more difficult to tell anyone what is happening. This kind of bullying can make you feel very lonely.

> Watch it! Whoops, did I hurt you?

▼ Whisper, Whisper

Saying nasty things behind your back can be very hurtful and is bullying. It's especially hard when someone is whispering horrible things to you without anyone else knowing what is going on.

> He's so stupid.

What do you know about bullying, Billy?

"When I got a mobile phone for Christmas I was really excited. Then this gang of older children pretended to be my friend and I gave them my mobile number. They started to send horrible text messages and called me names when they rang me up. They called me all sorts of names. I didn't know what to do. Then my friend told me to show a teacher some of the messages."

Who Gets Bullied?

Samuel is thinking about why he gets bullied. He worries that bullies pick on him because he reacts to being bullied, and gets upset. But bullies will pick on anyone they can get away with bullying. Bullying can happen to anyone, whether you are a boy or a girl, short or tall.

Small people get bullied…   …so do tall people.

I'm bigger than him but he really knows how to hurt me!

▼ Big Or Small

Bullies pick on anyone who they think is different from them, whether he or she is a different colour or from another culture, thin or fat, rich or poor. But we are all different from each other, in lots of ways. If you are bullied it is not your fault. Bullying is always wrong.

Alex, what is it like being bullied?

"When I was little I had a lisp. There was a boy in the year above me at school who was always picking on me. He would follow me around and copy the way I spoke. I began to really hate school. I would pretend to Mum that I was ill so I didn't have to go."

Who Bullies And Why?

There are lots of reasons why people bully others. Some people bully because it makes them feel important, others have been bullied themselves. Grace says you can't always tell if someone is a bully. Josie was bullied by someone who was smaller than she was, so it is not only big people who are bullies.

Both girls and boys can be bullies.

Some people bully so others will look up to them.

It's not always easy to spot a bully.

You can only play with us if you join our gang.

Story: Holly's Choice

1 Holly wanted to play with Marsha and her friends.

But first you have to prove yourself.

2 Marsha said Holly had to take Max's lunch money as a test before she joined.

This is wrong, but if I don't do it they'll pick on me.

3 Holly bullied Max while Marsha and the gang looked on.

Should Holly have taken the money?

No, it was stealing. There are lots of different types of gangs. Some are fun to be part of. Other gangs want you to prove that you are tough. They may ask you to bully someone before you can be in the gang. Some gangs try to make you do things you know are wrong. It is not always easy to say you won't go along with what is happening.

At my new school I'll be the first to bully.

▶ Tit For Tat

If you have been bullied at school, you may feel the only way to stop the bullying is to become a bully too. But you know what it feels like to be bullied. Do you really want others to feel the same?

Give me your pocket money!

I hate you. You're always pushing me around.

◀ Bullied At Home

Some people start to bully because they are being bullied at home, by a brother or sister or by a parent or carer. Adults can be bullies, too. Some bullies copy the way they see other people behave.

▶ It's Not Cool To Bully

Some people bully because they think it will win friends and make others admire them. But what sort of friends does a bully really have? Real friends are people who like being with you and having a good time, not people who are scared of you.

They all think I'm great!

▶ Feeling Jealous

Some people bully because they feel jealous of other people or their belongings, or because they feel no one likes them. But bullying is not the answer to any of these things.

▼ Taking It Out On Others

If you have been bullied you may feel angry. You may want to take it out on someone else. But it is never right to pick on others because you have been hurt.

You won't need that.

You won't need that.

Kylie, why did you begin to bully?

"My mum and dad never took much notice of me. They listened to my brother but never me. In the gang I used to bully to get people to notice me and listen to what I said. But my teacher found out about the bullying and spoke to Mum and Dad. We talked and things got better. I left the gang and found some new friends."

What Can Be Done?

Jason and his dad are talking about what can be done to stop bullying. When Jason was bullied he told the bully to leave him alone and walked away. His dad says it's important to tell an adult you trust, too. They will be able to help both the person being bullied and the bully.

Say "No!" to bullies.

Story: Should I Hit Back?

1 Paul was always being bullied by Mark. He didn't know what to do about it.

> Break it up! You two are in real trouble.

2 Paul's brother Barry said Paul should hit Mark back, but that might make things worse.

> If you don't stop, I'll tell a teacher.

3 Paul decided to stand up for himself and tell Mark to leave him alone.

What do you think of Barry's idea?

It is not easy to know what to do when you are being bullied. Some people say hitting back will stop the bullying, but you might get in trouble or be badly hurt. Try telling the bully to leave you alone. Practise what you are going to say until you feel confident. When you are bullied, say the words you have practised clearly and walk away.

Story: Laura Speaks Up

1 Laura saw Pete's gang bullying Jim.

Poor Jim. But if I try to help him they will turn on me.

2 After school Laura had a quiet word with Mrs Black.

Jim's being bullied but he's too scared to tell.

I'm glad you told me. We'll sort it out.

I'm sorry I bullied Jim. I'm unhappy because my dad hits me.

3 Mrs Black spoke to Pete and found out why he had started to bully others.

Was Laura right to tell?

Yes. It is hard to know what to do if you see someone being bullied. You might feel it has nothing to do with you, or be worried that you might get bullied too if you say anything. Find an adult you trust and tell them what is happening. Probably they will be able to stop the bullying without the bully knowing anyone has told.

> Leave her alone, Ryan. Sarah, come and play with us.

▶ Speak Up

If you see someone being bullied, think about how you can help them. Don't just stand by and let it carry on. Think how you would feel if it was happening to you.

◀ Getting Help

If you are being bullied, tell an adult. Think carefully about who to tell. It could be your mum, dad or carer, a teacher, classroom helper or a dinner lady. If the first person you tell does not take you seriously, go on telling until you find someone who will help you.

▶ Answer Back

Make a joke of things. Replies don't have to be very clever but it does help to have an answer ready. Practise saying your lines in the mirror at home. Good replies work best if the bully just needs to be put off. They might decide you are too clever to pick on.

Jason, how can you stop someone bullying you?

"You will need to judge the situation carefully. Fighting back won't help, so stay calm. You might try to ignore the bully. If you don't get upset, the bully might give up. You might stand up to the bully. But if you can't sort it out for yourself, tell an adult. Bullying is never right and bullies need help to stop bullying."

How Do You Feel?

Diane knows that when you are bullied you can feel angry or frightened, lonely, hurt, miserable or just confused. You may not want to eat anything. You may not be able to sleep, or you might have nightmares. When Diane was bullied she couldn't face school.

Bullies can make you angry.

Bullies can make you sad.

Being bullied made me miserable. I didn't know what to do.

Don't worry. It will be okay.

▶ It's Good To Talk

If you have been bullied, you will need to talk about how you feel. Keeping feelings inside can make it worse. Think about who you can talk to easily. It might be your friend, your mum or dad, sister, brother, or another adult.

▼ Being Different...

When you are being bullied, try to remember it is not your fault. The bully may have picked on something about you that is different, as an excuse to bully you. But everyone is different. Think about the good things about yourself and what you do well.

Diane, did you talk to anyone?

"I didn't tell anyone about the bullying for ages. I was miserable and scared, and I thought no one could help. Mum asked me what was wrong and even then it took ages to tell her. Mum spoke to the head of my school. He talked to the bully and the bullying stopped."

Bullies And Gangs

Most gangs are about friends being together, having a good time and doing the things they like. But some gangs put pressure on people to do things which they feel are wrong. It's not good to be part of that kind of gang, especially when they are bullies.

▼ Gangs Can Be Great!

It can be good to be part of a gang. It feels great to know that your friends are behind you, and support you whether you win or lose.

Hurry up, slowcoach!

Ignore him, you ran a great race.

Our gang really gets things done!

▲ Do The Right Thing

Sometimes it may be hard not to go along with what the gang is doing if you disagree. You may feel you will lose your friends if you won't be part of what is happening. But in the end you have to stand up for what you think is right.

Amy, is your gang fun?
"It's brilliant. Paula and I used to be in a different gang but they started bullying. We didn't feel right about it, so we left the gang and started our own. The bullies were annoyed but we kept out of their way and soon they stopped bothering us."

Don't Forget...

1

Did you talk to anyone, Alex?

"It's really horrible to be bullied. When you are being bullied it may be difficult to believe that it can ever stop. But bullying can only go on if the person being bullied keeps quiet about it. Tell an adult you trust. Tell your friends how you are feeling, too. Some people think bullying is part of growing up. But no one should put up with bullying."

2

What does your gang do together, Amy?

"We do loads of things – swimming, football, cinema trips. We look out for each other. Paula had a brilliant idea when we started the gang. Instead of bullying, we would watch out for people who were being bullied. If we see someone being bullied, we tell the bully to stop. If it's a gang we go and tell an adult who will help sort it out."

What does your school do about bullying, Jason?

"At my school we had a class discussion about bullying. We talked about what it felt like to be bullied and the bullies said how they were feeling, too. Bullies need help to think about other people's feelings as well as their own. They need to understand how their actions affect other people. Whatever the reason, it is always wrong to bully."

Diane, what are your tips for dealing with bullies?

"It's not easy to know what to do about bullying. Sometimes it's possible to stand up for yourself. Practise in front of a mirror first. If that doesn't work, tell a grown-up who can help. Don't be scared of telling, it is often the bravest thing to do."

Find Out More About Bullying

Helpful Addresses and Phone Numbers

Talking about problems can really help. If you can't talk to someone close to you, then try ringing one of these organisations:

Childline
Tel: 0800 1111
A 24-hour free helpline for children. The number won't show up on a telephone bill.

Kidscape
2 Grosvenor Gardens,
London SW1W 0DP
Tel: 020 7730 3300 (Mon-Fri 10am-4pm) A helpline for parents of bullied or bullying children. Send a large SAE for copies of their booklets.

NSPCC (National Society for the Prevention of Cruelty to Children)
Tel: 0800 800 500
A 24-hour free helpline for anyone worried about bullying.

Kids Helpline, Australia
Tel: 1800 55 1800
A 24-hour free helpline for children. Kids Helpline also offers online counselling either via the web or email at www.kidshelp.com.au

ParentLink, Australia
Tel: 02 6205 8800
A confidential helpline offering advice for parents of bullied or bullying children.

On the Web

These websites are also helpful.
You can get in touch with some
of them using email:

www.childline.org.uk

www.kidscape.org.uk

www.beatbullying.org

www.kidshealth.org

www.bullying.org

www.kidshelp.com.au

www.bullyingnoway.com.au

Further Reading

If you want to read more about
bullying, try:

Talking About Bullying by
Bruce Sanders (Aladdin/Watts)

How Can I Deal With Bullying by
Sally Hewitt (Franklin Watts)

I Feel Bullied by Jen Green (Hodder
Wayland)

The Bullybusters Joke Book by John
Byrne (Red Fox)

Picking on Percy by Cathy MacPhail

Bullying by Michelle Elliott (Wiseguides
series, Hodder Children's Books)

*Choices and Decisions: Dealing
With Bullying* by Pete Sanders and
Steve Myers (Aladdin/Watts)

Index

Photocredits

l-left, r-right, b-bottom, t-top, c-centre, m-middle

All photos from istockphoto.com except:

Cover tc, 6, 26 – DAJ. 9 — Brand X Pictures. 24 — Photodisc.

All the photos in this book have been posed by models.